Leaves from
Moon Mountain

Leaves from Moon Mountain

Moon Mountain Sangha
1719 Union Street
San Francisco, CA 94123
moonmountainsangha@sbcglobal.net
www.dorothyhunt.org

First Edition.

ISBN: 9780692521427

Collage art © by Rashani Réa
All rights reserved. www.rashani.com
Book Design: Cindy Chang
Cover Design: Rashani Réa

Leaves from Moon Mountain

Poems and Reflections
Dorothy Hunt

Collage Art
Rashani Réa

Moon Mountain Sangha Publishing, San Francisco

This book is dedicated
to my beloved husband, Jim

whose spirit has merged
with Moon Mountain

yet whose love continues
to pour forth from
the Heart we share

With deepest gratitude for

Ramana Maharshi
Adyashanti

and countless others
who light the Way

Adyashanti with author Dorothy Hunt

Contents

Truth can never be spoken.
Yet leaves fall unbidden
When the wind blows.

Leaves from Moon Mountain

Introduction

AS I SIT DOWN TO WRITE, it is a stunningly clear autumn day on Moon Mountain. Enormous California oak trees, their trunks and branches covered with moss, provide a canopy through which I see a brilliantly blue sky and a shower of leaves being blown in circles by the wind. Occasionally, an acorn falls, making a hollow sound as it hits the ground. This moment is like no other moment, and no matter how tenaciously the oak leaves may hold on to the tree, eventually they will fall. This is the movement of life.

While Moon Mountain may be only a tiny dot on a map, it is a reminder of something vast and profound. Zen masters have poetically described the Mystery that is awake in each of us as the moon of enlightenment, and this moon of enlightenment shines right through the mountain of form—all forms. It is reflected in the form of this mountain, the oak trees, the leaves that fall, the lizards that sun themselves on rocks here. This mystery is shining in your form and mine right here and now, whether we realize it or not.

The whirling leaves and the movement of thought are simply expressions of a deep and flowing mystery that includes birth and death, and what is beyond birth and death. Life's stream cannot be captured in a book, nor the boundless mystery described in words, yet creation moves.

The reflections, poems, and collages included in this book represent moments of life's flow. As much as words attempt to point beyond themselves to what cannot be described, they will ultimately fail, as all words must, being only dim shadows of Reality. And yet, when words and images are paired together, sometimes they can open the heart to that greater Reality that is always Now—a Reality that is timeless yet continually moving as time. In truth, we can hold on to nothing, neither yesterday's insight, nor a dream of tomorrow's awakening. That there is nothing to hold on to is both the mind's greatest fear and its eventual liberation.

Each moment contains the wholeness of a Mystery that cannot be known through the intellect, but can be intuited, sensed, felt in the heart of one's very being. Perhaps through Rashani's art and my words, the same Mystery that moves the wind and moves the creative spirit will touch that place in you that knows without words, that senses what is beyond sensing yet is present in the very ordinary moments of our lives.

Dorothy Hunt, 2015

A leaf floating
    on the wind

without time,
    without worry,
        without a destination.

        True surrender.

A Floating Leaf

A FLEETING IMAGE FROM A NATURE FILM that I saw many years ago touched me so deeply that it unexpectedly brought tears. Not only did I watch the film three times in the movie theaters particularly to see this one brief image, but I also bought the video when it became available so that I could pause it at the exact moment of the image. It was a simple image—that of a dry, curled leaf floating on water. Each time I saw the image, something stirred deeply and mysteriously in my being. To this day, whenever I see a leaf floating on a stream, in a river, or even floating down from a tree, something in me stops, and my heart seems flooded with an indescribable awe, and a sense of devotion.

What is it about this image of a floating leaf that resonates so deeply in my being? That brings a penetrating inner gasp? The bittersweet truth of impermanence? The beauty of autumn? It feels deeper than these. For me, this image speaks of life lived in freedom, in devotion to truth, and in surrender to the Mystery that moves life.

In my years as a seeker, I wrote many letters to my teachers. I did not know why I frequently enclosed a leaf before mailing them. One day I happened upon a passage from the Bhagavad-Gita (9:26-27) that said "any offering—a leaf, a flower, fruit, a cup of water" would be accepted by the divine if given from a loving heart. It spoke of the surrendered life as giving everything—whatever we say, eat, pray, enjoy, or suffer—to the divine.

What I did not understand consciously when I first felt so moved by a floating leaf seems more apparent now. The leaf was seeing itself as leaf; the wholeness of being was seeing itself whole; the seeker who was so deeply touched by the image of a floating leaf was the Mystery stirring, in its human expression, the longing for truth, freedom, and surrender of the illusion of separation. How each of us is aroused to awaken, to aspire for enlightenment, comes in many forms. But the deep longing for truth, God, Self, awakening comes from within Itself, your Self. Nothing is outside your Self—not a leaf or a galaxy, longing or loving, a god or a guru.

For a time, we may bow before an idea, an image, a form, a picture, a deity, a teacher, a guru, a mountain, imagining that is divine and we are not. Eventually, we discover it is only the divine that sees the divine; it is only a buddha who sees a buddha. In an instant of awakening, we see that what we had previously sought outside, was all the time Seeing from inside. It is right to offer everything to the Mystery—by whatever name—not because it is demanded or a holy thing to do, but because it belongs to its true Source and has never belonged to a "me."

Just as the leaf does not ask why the wind is blowing from one direction and not another, a life lived in harmony with Reality does not refuse the moment-to-moment unfolding of life. In our being at-one with our true nature, we are intimately at-one with the moment that is here Now. This intimacy actualizes our freedom, compassion, love, and wisdom.

What is a floating leaf? Simply a floating leaf! Life needs no meaning to be what it is, and yet Truth seems to conceal or reveal itself moment to moment. Be intimate with the moments of your own experience. Pay attention to those that seem to touch you in some deep, unknown, mysterious place. Who knows how the Infinite will dance today?

Each moment
the Unconditioned shines
right through the conditioned.

月山

The moon of enlightenment
reveals itself
in this mountain of form.

Moon Mountain

WHEN MY SPIRITUAL TEACHER, Adyashanti, invited me to share the dharma in 2004, I knew that eventually I wanted to form a non-profit organization to support the teachings and retreats that I would offer to others interested in Awakening.

For years, the name eluded me. Then one day, my husband and I looked at property in Sonoma, California on Moon Mountain. We were drawn to the peacefulness of the land and its views, the sprawling oaks and moss-covered boulders, and the simplicity of the home nestled there among the trees. I knew immediately that, whether our offer on the property was accepted or not, I had found the name I had been searching for: Moon Mountain Sangha.

When we returned home later that day, and I opened my computer, there was the photograph that had been my screen saver for years and years. The photo was of a moon and a mountain. I had been looking at the moon and the mountain every single day!

Like Awakening itself, sometimes it takes a long time to discover that what we were looking for, what we longed for, what we hoped to find *someday* was right in front of us and right within us all along—so close we did not even notice! In fact, it is looking out of our eyes this very moment.

In Zen, the moon is frequently used as a symbol for enlightenment and the mountain a symbol for form. So Moon Mountain also seemed a perfect name for the recognition that the "moon of enlightenment" resides right here in this "mountain of form." Form and the formless are simply *not two*. We, and the world around us, are Spirit through and through, and have never been divided except in thought. Yet it is only in stillness and silence, not delivered by thought, that we receive the grace of this knowing, which is our *being*.

Our family now has a home on Moon Mountain, literally and figuratively. Sometimes the moon seems close enough to touch here, and the last thing you hear before falling asleep is a soothing lullaby sung by crickets and the wind. But deeper than all appearances is the limitless moon of enlightenment that, as Zen Master Dogen once noted, is reflected wholly and completely even in a single dewdrop.

When we sit, stand, or walk in our true nature, we may feel the great Silence in our own form as a mountain—firm, unshakable, deeply rooted in the mysterious Ground, the unnamable Source of all. This vast Mystery shows up as this very life in form. Totally wondrous that out of darkness, light emerges; out of sleep, we awaken; right in form is the formless; out of all that is impermanent, we discover the timelessness of each moment!

A mountain of Silence
resounds within.
Be still and listen.

When we simply stop!
and notice what is here,
there is no mountain to climb.
There is only Now.

What is unborn and undying
        unfurls itself
            a tender shoot in spring
                a petal falling in summer
                    a dry leaf in autumn
                        a bare branch in winter.

White-washed walls
hold images of winter persimmons,
maple leaves beginning to unfurl.

Here, I rake gravel,
drink tea, walk barefoot
across wooden floors.

LONGING FOR NOTHING

Alone on Moon Mountain
there is great peace,
longing for nothing.

Mu and Kannon
spring up laughing
from this rock-strewn ground.

There is a sea of green here—
tender shoots, moss,
the oaks, my heart.

White-washed walls
hold images of winter persimmons,
maple leaves beginning to unfurl.

Here, I rake gravel,
drink tea, walk barefoot
across wooden floors.

Memories of Japan linger here—
mist-enshrouded mountains,
tall pines, this daffodil.

Suddenly I long for the fragrance
of incense, the sound of my teacher's
black robes and silent feet.

But Zen has jumped off
the cushion of ceremony and formal bows,
of bald heads sitting motionless.

Now I meet with ordinary buddhas
on Moon Mountain.
We stop and listen to the wind.

And here it is again;
the great peace,
longing for nothing.

The moon is already full,
shining from your own eyes,
illuminating the Way.

DAWN ON MOON MOUNTAIN

Out of darkness,
black silhouettes emerge
from the hushed light
of a pale gray sky.

Oaks stand unmoving
in a vast stillness.
The wind is not yet awake,
yet something listens

deeply, intimately,
to pink and orange
speaking
Silence.

CHANGING WEATHER

Weather changes on the
mountain
as it does in our form.
Thoughts, feelings, moods—
changing weather.
While there are many
causes and conditions
for the movement
of our time-bound mind,
Truth has none.
It is timeless and will,
of itself,
reveal its true face
as our own.

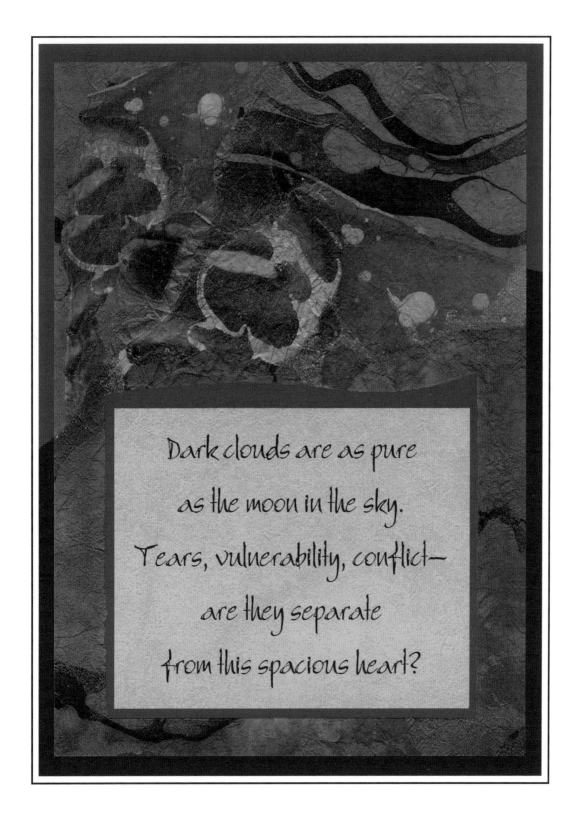

Dark clouds are as pure
as the moon in the sky.
Tears, vulnerability, conflict—
are they separate
from this spacious heart?

Sit as a mountain.
Flow as a river.
Be open as the sky.
Your true Heart
will lead the way.

Eventually Silence will draw us
deeper and deeper into the Mountain.
But be forewarned:
Those who have deeply entered
Moon Mountain
do not return;
yet they walk and talk
and move about in the world
as though they have.

You do not become enlightened.
You are Enlightenment itself.

無

Truth is its own knowing.
It needs no knower.

Truth

ULTIMATE TRUTH CANNOT BE KNOWN BY THE INTELLECT. It cannot be spoken in words. It cannot be made into an object, though countless beings have tried. Truth belongs to no religion, no scripture, no philosophy. Yet it is what we all are, what the world is, what moves this moment, and what lies beyond all appearances and all dualities. We use words such as timeless, formless, spirit; mystery, emptiness, infinite potential; nondual awareness, being, God—but none of these words can actually capture their Source.

When the mind is quiet enough, ventures close enough, is withdrawn deeply enough toward the Unknown and seems about to touch its Source, it can no longer remain separate. In that moment, it is subsumed. What knows Itself cannot be known by the mind, and yet reveals Itself in silence and stillness. When the mind re-emerges, returning to its limited subject/object consciousness, it can never truly describe the experience to another, yet something remains "known" forever in the Heart. A single moment of awakening has the potential to transform the apparent trajectory of our lives.

Such moments, empty of definition, are akin to deep and dreamless sleep. When we are not dreaming, there is no self, no world, no other, no God, and yet we do not imagine we have died each night. What can we say when there is no content knowable to the mind? And yet... many have tasted, or been awakened by grace, to such moments of deep and mysterious remembrance of our true nature, its emptiness and oneness with every expression of life.

In the aftermath, we may realize that truly there is nothing to be taught, nothing to impart. Our essence is what has always been awake. There is only uncovering the conditioned beliefs, judgments, feelings, and fears that appear to obscure the Truth that has awakened itself within us.

Most spiritual seekers are not seeking the dissolution of an illusory separate self. Most are initially seeking a blissful experience, relief from suffering, or an antidote to a fear of death. This is not a bad thing, but as Truth begins to pull our consciousness inward, we realize that what began as a "me" seeking truth, God, enlightenment, or an end to suffering, is actually being disarmed, dismantled, and subtracted back to zero. Here the mind often becomes fearful and may distract itself endlessly from such a movement.

And yet, you may be one of those fortunate souls deeply called to the Truth that sets us free.

Ultimate Truth supports the discovery of relative truth as well. When we see things as they actually are, and not as our mind has been conditioned to see—through its judgments, biases, prejudices, and fears—we are free even in the midst of conflict, grief, confusion, bickering neighbors or politicians, or the experience called dying.

When our relative truth is aligned with the movement of ultimate Truth, we feel life flowing. When we try to make a conceptual box out of either, stuffing one concept into another, we feel limited and contracted. When we are in resistance to life as it is, our bodies show us by our tension, anxiety, and anger at not being in control. Truth reveals those moments clearly, with no judgment whatsoever, but out of Love. When we allow untruth to be touched by Truth, when what is unloved is touched by Love, transformation begins to happen on its own.

Sit quietly.
Strip off the masks
of self-deception,
self-reflection,
self-improvement,
self-judgment.
If you want truth,
these activities waste energy.

Sit quietly.
What is peering out
from behind your mask?
Without relying on a single thought,
who are you?
No matter what you see,
there is more unseen.
Always, the Mystery invites itself deeper.

What is there to seek?
What is there to find?
What is truth?
What is not truth?
Nothing is.
Nothing is not.
What, then, is there to do
Or not do?

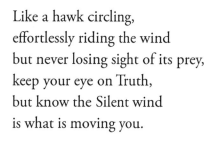

Like a hawk circling,
effortlessly riding the wind
but never losing sight of its prey,
keep your eye on Truth,
but know the Silent wind
is what is moving you.

Ten thousand clouds
Do not diminish the vast sky.

Ten thousand thoughts
Do not diminish timeless Truth.

Truth is never separate
from its own movements.
That is why it is so intimate
with the moment.

When we are being truth,
we are not seeking it.
When we are truly interested in understanding,
we are not demanding to be understood.
When we are being love,
we are not defending our hearts
or requiring others to love us.
When we are deeply listening,
we are not waiting to be heard.

Thoroughly investigate the question,
Who am I?
When this question is resolved,
it will render all other questions
irrelevant.

When Silence reveals Truth,
there is nothing outside.
The whole world is inside

YOU.

What is looking

through your eyes?

Thinking cannot see.
Seeing reveals thinking.

When you live in Unknowing,
you are available for
Truth to move
freely.

Before there was a word,
where was separation?
Now that there are words,
where is separation?

TELL THE TRUTH

Tell the truth!
Your mind does not know how to love.
Tell the truth!
Your mind does not know how to surrender.
Tell the truth!
Your mind does not know how
to keep the planets in their orbits
or make leaves let go in winter,
or bring new blossoms in the spring.
Tell the truth!
Your mind does not know how to truly live,
or let go into death.
But You do.
Trust Yourself.

Do you want truth more than you want life to look a certain way?
Do you want truth more than you want your "own" life?
Do you want to know the truth inside your bones and marrow?
Then you must ask your Heart its deepest questions.

Truth does not ask
our mind's permission to move;
it simply moves.
When it does, it can create or destroy,
but it does so in the service of itself,
not in the service of a "me."

Every moment
is the truth;
but to choose
the truth
in every moment
might take lifetimes
of devotion
yet can only happen
Now.

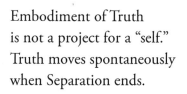

Embodiment of Truth
is not a project for a "self."
Truth moves spontaneously
when Separation ends.

You can never figure out
how to embody Truth.
Truth embodies you
when you have subtracted
yourself back to zero.
Even then, you can never
see your own shining.

You
can only
BE what you
are.

Silence thunders as the

mountain shakes loose its green.

Sky is breathing

an intense blue breath

rising and falling with the wind.

Stillness settles all disputes

with birdsongs.

40

Silence

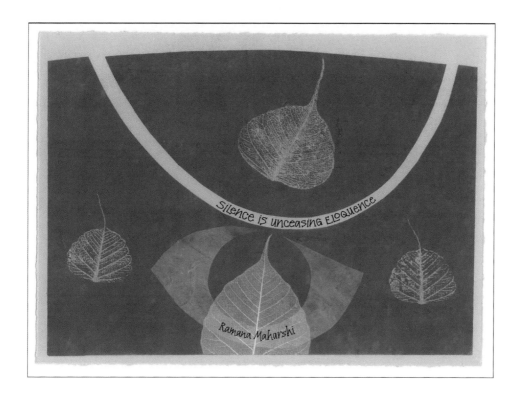

Silence is unceasing eloquence

Ramana Maharshi

MANY YEARS AGO, Ramana Maharshi appeared to me in a dream. I did not know who he was, whether he was dead or alive, or what he taught. But the peaceful, loving look on his face, the luminous Presence flowing out of his eyes drew me into a silence that seemed to reveal a depth I had not previously known existed. After several years of spontaneous self-inquiry *(Who is sitting here? Who is feeling anxious? Who is looking at herself in the mirror? Who am I?)*, the mind stopped long enough to receive the truth of what I am, what you are, what the whole world is—even though no words can capture Truth. Spiritual inquiry can deliver us instantly back to Silence. In this Silence, everything, nothing, love, emptiness, awakeness, mystery, and the "is-ness" of the moment merge in a single seeing/knowing that contains absolutely no concepts.

Silence is a deep, interior Presence and absence of "self" that actually has nothing to do with whether there is noise or quiet in the environment or in the mind. What is revealed in Silence is your Being, your Presence, your awake and intimate Awareness that makes it possible to see, listen, taste, touch, smell, think, and to experience what is beyond the senses and the thinking mind. While each thing has its own quality of Silence, in its deepest dimension, this Silence is what we are, what life is, what moves the universe and simultaneously is its Source.

The deeper the Silence, the greater is the felt sense of the Mystery that sees beyond all thoughts, images, and acquired knowledge. We become aware of a deeper dimension of our Being that is very quiet, very still, completely open, very natural. The mind may be chattering away, music may be playing, and emotions may be emoting. But still, the silent ground is felt as a quiet, alive presence that is not separated from experience and yet not affected by it, either.

Psychologically minded folks may wonder if soaking in Silence is a way of bypassing what needs to be seen or felt or understood. In the true Silence of our awake nature, nothing is avoided, nothing denied, nothing attached. Rather than numbing us to experience, this Silence lovingly invites everything that has been hidden or denied to come out of the shadows into the light. True Silence opens us to the truth of the present moment.

One does not have to effort to find this Silence and Stillness. It is not something we create. It is felt the moment we relax and become receptive, the moment we stop trying to move toward or away from anything.

Moving toward is not needed.

Moving away is not needed.

Everything is here

without separation.

A journey with no distance,
A mystery with no end—
Simple, unadorned,
Unwavering, unflappable
Free from attachments
Possessing nothing
Being nothing
Wanting nothing
Attaining nothing.
In its Silence
All things end
And also begin—
Each breath,
Each thought,
Each moment.

Soaking
in silence is like
being bathed from the inside out.

Whatever needs attention, warmth,
love, purification, liberation, is invited
forth from the shadows to be seen,
felt, drawn back into the
wholeness that belongs
to our Being.

This unknowable Mystery is silent.
Listen!
crickets chirping
bees humming
doves cooing
dogs barking
leaves rustling
streams gurgling
petals opening
clouds colliding
children giggling
Nothing else but Silence sounding.

Listen deeply to Silence.
Its subtle sound,
its quiet vibration
beckons us Home.

ℰ∂

Be the Silence,
not the one who is silent.
Be the Presence,
not the one trying to be present.
Be the Awareness,
not the one being aware.

ℰ∂

When no one is aware of silence,
there is Silence.
When the meditator has disappeared,
there is true meditation.

Reality never struggles with its life—
yet can move as thoughts
that seem to.
From its own unceasing Silence,
this moment appears.
What is it? Who can say?

&

Silence fills all cracks,
Opening out to nothing.

&

This Silence is empty.
What is empty is silent,
yet this Silence is empty
of nothing.

LOOK IN THE MIRROR

Look in the mirror at your own face.
Do you see the light streaming from your eyes?
Tell me, friend,
Are you the mirror or the seeing?
The reflection or the streaming light?
Look, look closely.

Look in the mirror of your own mind.
Look deeply
Past thought-waves and memory,
Past judgments and conclusions,
Liking or disliking.
Keep looking.

Look in the mirror of your own awareness,
Clear, serene,
Untouched-touching
Unchanging-ever-changing
Unmoving-ever-moving
Deep water-awareness.

Gaze into what you do not know.
Be steady. Do not flinch.
You long to know what's true before you die,
But knowing will be your death.
Which will it be?

Fear bubbles in the shadows.
Distractions, control, rage
Rise up to protect an image
That has not been the friend
You hoped.
You are looking for the True Friend.

Standing on the edge,
Trembling open,
You think there is something to do.
But all that is required is to
Be still.
Be still and know.

Look into the Round Mirror
Unnameable darkness,
Streaming light radiance.
Look so deeply into your self
Your image disappears.
Now what are you?

Silence does not answer.

Each sees the mystery
uniquely,

yet the Mystery
is what sees.

54

Mystery

THE MYSTERY OF OUR UNDIVIDED BEING CAN ONLY BE EXPERIENCED. When we try to find it by thinking, we create a concept, an object, a division where there is none. When we touch into the undivided state, we realize we do not know who we are. We become a mystery to ourselves.

Absent of qualities, yet intimate with each tiny leaf, each speck of dust, each galaxy in the universe, and each one of us, this Mystery swallows opposites in a single gulp. The thought called "me," looking for the unknown, unborn, and unconditioned, is like a candle looking for the sun. It will melt as it draws near. The thought of who we are cannot maintain separation in the face of what we truly are.

When the mind is consumed by this Mystery, thoughts disappear momentarily; ideas and images are swallowed up. This serene Darkness of Unknowing leaves nothing outside of itself, and simultaneously allows nothing and no one to enter. It is impossible to describe this imageless space, this profound Abyss that empties everything into Itself. This Mystery speaks no words, has no thoughts, needs no understanding, has no will, and assumes no form. Everything you ever imagined about God, Self, enlightenment, or ignorance ends. In fact, "you" end.

Here there is no seeking, no perfecting, no deepening. Experiences of peace, bliss, freedom, presence, insight, and understanding are rendered irrelevant. Here, in the words of the Christian mystic Meister Eckhart, is where "distinction never gazed."

Yet, right out of this dark Mystery shines the light of our own Awakeness that both illumines and continually moves the whole of life in its many forms. The Mystery appears to create out of itself everything that is, including the experience of space and time that are necessary for the appearance of life in form and the sense of duration. It appears to do this in a manner similar to our nighttime dreams—creating out of its own Consciousness universes and forms that can move, feel, be born, and die. The causes and conditions of this very moment being exactly as it is are vast, and depend on the continual flowing of an undivided Whole.

When this Mystery moves to wake itself up out of identification with its dream of "me," there is no "one" who awakens. Although the dream itself continues, the Mystery has awakened to itself. There is nothing to know, and no state to be maintained; this is the non-state in which all states arise and return.

In the presence of the silent Mystery, we lose our arrogance—the assumption that we "know" something. In the face of the Mystery, we are humbled. Mind becomes a servant of truth rather than a seeker or a finder.

BREAKING THROUGH

Listen! Listen beyond your listening.
Listen! Listen beyond God's listening.
Do you know the words
You and *God* are creations?
Truth is not a word.

Sit! Sit in Yourself before creation.
Sit! before you had a place to sit.
Be! before you spoke being or non-being,
before you wanted, before you knew,
before you had somewhere for truth to move.

There is no place for you and God to meet.
Instrumentality is a figment of imagination.
Keep going deeper, before you had a mind
to question, before you had a mind to know.
Keep going deeper; do not stop.

Do not stop until you're stopped,
dissolved beyond your thoughts of what dissolves.
Do not stop until there's nothing left that
even knows itself to have a will,
neither a "my" will nor a "God's" will.

Now that is poverty; and the thought
called "me" that is searching for some riches
will want to avoid such poverty at all costs.
But you have come here to listen, to sit, to be,
and to move as a Mystery that isn't even moving.

Now! Now is the time for breaking through.
It is neither your break-through nor God's.
Breaking through is what breaks through.
Who knows how? Who knows where?
Who knows the mind that is Unborn?

What is aware
of both presence and absence?

THAT is the hiding place
of true liberation.

PRIOR TO LIGHT

Here, in this darkness prior to light
where the world disappears
in its own vast nothingness,
eyes cannot see, mind cannot know.
There is no consolation of God
or self, or other, nor is there terror,
even though the mind is like a
deep, black swirling, moving
without direction or purpose.

Sleep is not possible here
although nothing is awake.
Here, in the unborn silence,
everything that took itself
to be divine or human
collapses in on itself
into a poverty like none other.
Even nakedness is removed
along with will or knowing.

There is no meaning to these words,
no freedom paired with bondage.
To be God's instrument makes no sense.
This is prior to God, prior to creation,
prior to light, the endpoint of all desires,
and also their beginning.
A philosopher might ask who is aware,
but he does not yet know himself
prior to light, for if he did,
there could be no questions.

DISSOLVING

Coming…Going
Creation…Destruction
Emptiness…Fullness
Freedom…Bondage.

Come to where these words dissolve.

Here you will find neither
Duality…nor Nonduality
Ignorance…nor Enlightenment
Purity…nor Impurity
Time…nor the Absence of time.

Here, nothing is
Attached...or Detached
Known...or Unknown
Asleep...or Awake
Divided...or Undivided.

Here, the mind cannot speak.
No you…No me
No union…No separation
No form…No formlessness
No death…No deathlessness.

Silence alone reveals what thought cannot think
What knowing cannot know,
What listening cannot hear,
What seeing cannot see.

Here, time and timelessness,
space and no space, you and other
presence and absence
collapse into a single flowing.

Here, there is no fear
but no sense of safety,
Here, there is no doubt, yet
no one who is certain.

Here there are no distinctions,
yet the uniqueness of each thing,
each moment, each breath
reveals the Mystery.

DEEPER, STILL DEEPER

The Heart's Mystery
can neither be spoken nor thought,
but can be touched in Silence
where everything whispers its presence.

The deeper and quieter the listening,
the more Silence reveals itself as Source—
unnamable, unspeakable,
indescribable, yet so intimate ... Now.

What is always awake
can sometimes appear to be asleep,
until a birdsong, a temple bell, a single moment
reminds us of where we've always been.

Here, time and timelessness,
space and no space, you and Other
presence and absence
collapse into a single flowing.

Here, there is no fear
but no sense of safety,
Here, there is no doubt, yet
no one who is certain.

Here there are no distinctions,
yet the uniqueness of each thing,
each moment, each breath
reveals the Mystery.

Listen beyond your listening.
Be still beyond Stillness.
Let the moment arrive without
   interpretation;
let it return without grasping.

You long to know the Heart's Mystery.
The Mystery moves your longing.
Enough words. Let Silence take you
where the mind cannot go.

Deeper, still deeper.

Blackness behind a mirror,
unseen—
yet without it,
no image is reflected.

Likewise,
behind reflected appearances—
a dark Mystery where
opposites meet, merge, and
completely disappear.

In deeply perceiving
both the wholeness and
flowing of this Mystery,
there is no blaming, shaming,
fearing or separating ourselves
from any aspect of that wholeness.

Minds make meaning
where none exists:
There is no end.

Minds make meaning
where none exists.
There is no end.

Mind

WHEN I SPEAK HERE OF MIND, I am referring primarily to that aspect of human consciousness that manifests as thought and perception, and includes memory, feeling, will, imagination, and reflection. This particular movement of the Mystery reflects on the perception of the senses (which are essentially thoughtless and timeless) and ascribes meaning and time to them. It remembers and can also contemplate its own thought-creations. It is, essentially, a movement of thought reflecting upon a collection of information, including information about the physical body, the environment, and the behavior of other forms.

Most human beings take this movement of thought and perception to be an identity, a self-organizing principle called "me," around which all other movements revolve. What begins as an innocent and functionally necessary sense of self in a young child evolves into a vast array of concepts that are taken to be a defined and separate "self," separate from *being*, separate from world, separate from other forms, and even separate from itself (as when a thought called "I" judges or reflects upon another thought called "myself.")

The alive, aware sense of being, which we all share as our common reference, "I," turns into a concept of "I," an "I-thought" that is felt energetically as a "knot," an intermediary between Consciousness and the body that actually has no independent existence but "thinks" it does. It is important to note that the "sense" of self is neither an enemy to defeat nor an obstacle to liberation. The obstacle is identification with what we are not.

Consciousness, fused or identified with a conditioned body/mind, is what is called ego, but "ego" has no actual existence. It is a word ascribed to a movement of thought that separates itself from our wholeness and is experienced as an energetic field of resistance to what is. It manifests as effort, tension, thought, contraction, and a will to control that motivates our waking lives and carries an enormous emotional attachment. An ever-chatting inner commentator holds itself separate from Life and continually believes that things should be other than they are. When mind is identified with a self-image, it will always feel or fear a sense of lack because we have identified with something limited, conditioned, and continually at the mercy of others' perceptions. Our true nature has no sense of lack and no fear of non-existence.

Mind is an incredible tool, necessary and useful for functioning in this relative world; it just does not happen to be an identity, nor do its memories or projections define what we are. When we cease attaching "me" and "mine" to the movements of mind or emotion, we are free from the vast amount of suffering created when we blame a "me" or "other me's" for all kinds of things the "me" does not wish to experience. Ego is a movement to survive as a psychological entity that the self-reflecting mind has made into a noun. The inborn biological instinct for physical survival is distinguished from the ego's movement to survive as a separate center of the universe.

When we inquire deeply, *Who* or *What am I?*, we are asking the mind to find its Source. When the mind comes close to the edge of thought, close to the Unknown, it either contracts itself back into the known, or it melts into Being. Awakening is a profound shift from egoic identity to the Mystery that is awake in us all.

Busy mind is like an insect buzzing at your window.
If you weren't awake, how would you notice?

Mind is like a bird, continually hopping
from thought-branch to thought-branch
on a tree called "me."
Uproot the me-thought.
Free your mind!

Mind is the hunter.
Mind is the prey.
Mind is the Buddha.

Not-knowing mind
is the mind of enlightenment.

Life seems to ask for many decisions,
but really, it is making them.
Sometimes your mind leans left, but you turn right.
A thought is nodding, but the clarity is "No."
Life moves itself without mind telling it how.
Since you are life, trust your movement,
knowing that
Resistance is futile.

Books close.

Questions cease.

Your own mind becomes the sutra.

Your own eyes transmit

light.

WHAT MEANING DO YOU MAKE OF THIS?

Tell me, friend, what meaning do you make of this:

That there have been wars since the beginning of time,
that despite thousands of years of religions, beings are not free?
that life flows in darkness and in light without an explanation?

Does a star plunging through the vast expanse
of endless sky need meaning to exist?
What about the fragrance of a rose, or rotting flesh
in streets where bombs have strewn body parts?

Tell me, friend, is there a need for meaning for
life to move, dreams to appear, or compassion to arise?
Gather all the books in all the lands, the beauty and the
horror they describe.

Is a single word that's spoken or story that is told
the experience of Now?
Minds make meaning where none exists, but
what is here without additions from your mind?

Choice
or no choice?
Avoid philosophical debate.
Love simply
loves.

How limiting our thoughts.
How vast our being!
Do we choose to stay secure,
asleep in the virtual reality
of our mind, or will we
choose to live awake
by stepping
into the Unknown?

Mind will never destroy itself.
The desire to do so
is more mind.

What is naked does not mind
how it is dressed.
Self or no-self—
both are
clothing.

LONGING AND LIBERATION

Oh mind! What prisons you make!
Fences made of concepts,
flimsy as a passing thought,
become steel bars in your imagination,
and you are trapped within yourself
longing for liberation!

Ideas of bondage and freedom,
ignorance and enlightenment,
darkness and light hold you hostage
in a world you cannot leave,
separate from a world you cannot enter.
Do you not see that longing is liberation?

The freedom that you seek is Who you are!
Here and now, in this moment as it is.
That which keeps the planets in their orbits
keeps you in yours, and created thoughts as well.
Oh mind! Seek your Source, not your limitation!
You are wild and free just inches from ideas.

What if there is no prisoner inside your thoughts?

Creation comes from the Mystery,
seizes us when it does,
commands and demands our attention,
heightens our awareness,
and touches our heart
until it pours forth.

Creation

CREATION IS A VAST AND MARVELOUS EXPRESSION OF BEING. That leaves unfurl in spring and let go in autumn; that the bark of each tree is unique; that the moss on the rocks of Moon Mountain contain hundreds of life forms; that birds know how to sing, fly, build nests, and care for their young; that rivers find their way to the Ocean; that there are billions of galaxies in vast space; that you and I are living and breathing, aware of it all—is not Creation a miracle?

Of course there are many creations. We may find Mother Nature's creations beautiful or awe-inspiring, but imagine our body/minds are separate from Nature, and thus embark on an endless task of self-judgment, self-improvement, efforting to fix a "self" that we deem deficient. We may try to train our minds with punishment, rather than become curious about what our mind actually is and how it functions, how it continually creates stories and dramas to entertain itself, creates problems where none exist, and then embarks on the task of solving them.

Compassion moves in the face of suffering—whether it is an individual or the earth that appears in need of love. But the greatest suffering is caused by not knowing what we truly are. In demanding that life's moment-to-moment "creations" be other than they are, we struggle against life, against nature, and guess which wins—Life or your thoughts about it?

Then there is the creation of the Arts—the pull toward beauty, innovation, expression of a deep creative urge. Poets, painters, musicians, dancers; writers, designers, sculptors, gardeners, architects; and countless others creating works of art. No one knows why or how one is seized to create, but when the Mystery moves to create something from the human mind and heart, it won't let go until creation happens. It appears that Creation is a continual movement of Spirit as it pours itself into form. Mountains and paintings both arise right out of Silence.

As I write this, a large black and yellow butterfly flits by my window. Its life may be measured in days or even hours, but it fulfills its destiny to simply Be. Tiny flowers bloom in the cracks of city sidewalks. Daisies do not seem to fret that they are not roses. Only the human mind unfavorably compares its expression to others. If only we understood that the One shows up as all forms, all moments, all colors, shapes, and expressions of Creation. The flea is no less the One than enlightening beings. A single raindrop is no less the One than the vast Ocean.

We are the vast Ocean of Consciousness, creating out of itself all currents of life's movements, all waves on the surface of the sea. Do not think of yourself as separate from Nature's creation or from the Infinite Awakeness that is aware of Itself everywhere it looks.

THIS that you are is
      an infinitely mysterious Sea

That may offer buoyancy for your boat
      or a shattering storm.

It may deliver coolness for parched lips
      or leave you impossibly thirsty;

Be the wave that holds your surfboard,
      or the one that carries a shark.

Its blue-green water may soothe a troubled mind,
      or its ink-black darkness invite fear.

Its continual motion pulls you into an
      intense curiosity that drives your search:

What IS it—this mysterious Ocean
      holding the mystery of what I am?

And so you begin—at first tentatively,
      wading, barely tasting,

Then swimming with ease, sometimes gulping,
      diving and surfacing again and again,

Until finally, in utter silence, you dive so deeply
      neither you nor your questions remain.

Creation is a love letter from the One that has no end.

The impulse to create is one way
we are "made in the image of God."
True creativity is always at one with its creation.

Look deeply at any aspect of creation—
a mountain, a stone, a single blade of grass,
the eyes of a stranger, your own hand.
Feel the stillness that exists in the Awareness
that is looking and in what is seen.
When there is no separation, anything
can seem beautiful, even a cigarette butt
or an empty bag tossed on the street.

Consciousness is endlessly creating form.
The power of creation is within you.

What is your mind creating today?
Sad stories, happy stories, melodramas,
crushing defeats, glorious victories,
stories about a (non-existent) self
doing life right or wrong?
What if none of them were true?

We create the world we live in by how we see it.

No one possesses the jewel
and no one lets go;
yet buds come
and leaves fall endlessly.

ON A COUNTRY ROAD THE POPPIES BLOOM

On a country road the poppies bloom
in the grass between the tire tracks.
No one told them they should move
or save their beauty for another time,
or fear their life will end too soon.
They simply grow wherever they are,
and bloom when it's time, and die
when it's time, and never think
of asking why.

STILLNESS

Stillness!
        duck wings flap overhead
        flies zoom round an invisible track.

Stillness!
        tiny helicopters touch down on water
        their blue and white stripes
        glistening in the sun.

Silence!
        listening to cattails,
        oar sliding into water.

Peace.
        water still; reflections clear
        purple shirts, straw hats.
        Is there one, or are there two?

Peace.
        Not needing
        another moment.
        This one is it!

Conditioning is not an enemy.
What would a sunflower
or a maple tree be
without conditioning?

The tear that just fell on the ground
is this moment's raindrop.

Potter, who feels the touch of the clay?
Painter, what sees the color?
Singer, whose breath sustains your notes?
Poet, from where do words arise?

I AM

I am
the dragonfly flitting,
call of wild geese,
rustle of cattails,
parched desert earth,
coolness of a lake,
searing heat of noonday sun.

I am
confusion of mind,
tears of grief,
pain of longing,
joy of finding,
soft feathers of the owl
lying headless on pine needles.

I am
the song in your heart,
tears where you are touched,
clarity of Awareness,
Love melting
frozen feelings
and static beliefs.

I am
birth and death,
ongoing flow of Life eternal,
moon rising, sun setting,
undivided. I am Now.
I am You.
I am This!

WINTER RETURN

Winter return—
Empty and unadorned,
Bare-bones; trees
Silhouetted against cold sky,
Migrating wings hastening
Then disappearing.

Winter darkness—
Storm clouds, swirling gusts,
Silver grass leaning into solitude;
Stillness, turning, returning,
Each quiet breath warming
The dark face of Silence.

Radiant Mystery—ever-returning,
Unseen roots far beneath the mind
Flowing, freezing, thawing, dying
Into This! that has no tongue.
Hush! Listen deeply!
Can you hear the Soundless echo?

For This! You split in two—
to see Yourself
within your own creation.

Love is the reason,
without reason,
before reason,
its own reason,
no reason.

Yet here you are, Unborn,
unconditionally loving what dies.

Love

IT IS ONLY FROM THE DEEPEST MYSTERY OF SILENCE that love begins to truly flower. We cannot pry Love's petals open, or demand to receive love from others; but when we dwell as the Mystery of our own Being, love begins to reveal itself, and to move to meet itself in our own lives. While the flavors of love are many, its essence is One. Do we search for flavors or return to essence? Are we looking for love or being love?

Like a flower, love is rooted in the ground, the ground of our Being. It may not be noticed while its roots are growing deeper, being nurtured by the silence of our true nature, but at some point, its sends out a shoot, and we notice. We find ourselves more generous of spirit, no longer keeping score in relationships, more interested in deeply understanding others than in judging them. We watch our own hearts open and move in compassionate ways without the direction or manipulation of mind.

Love longs for itself in the human heart, but we imagine we are longing for something or someone "out there," a specific form, instead of the Love we are. The mind imagines that we only long for something we lack; but we do not long for anything we have not already known; we may be curious, but we do not feel a longing. Follow the deep longing for love back to its Source. Love may be longed for and simultaneously feared, for in the deepest love, there is no "other;" we have moved beyond the mind's illusion of separation.

Love has been defined in countless ways, but when it is moving selflessly, spontaneously, and unconditionally, there is no name or definition required or even possible, yet it is deeply felt. There is an intimacy with life, an acceptance of what is, an openness and a heartfelt desire for the well-being of all. Such unconditional love is indiscriminate, a love that only loves, regardless of circumstance. It has no requirement that we be worthy, perfected, or saintly. It is a love that does not know how to do anything but give itself, receive itself, touch its own confusion and suffering with a tender compassion that continually points back to Itself, if we have eyes to see.

When we open our hearts to the love that is knocking from the inside, the love waiting to be let *out*, we begin to discover the huge presence of love within us. Layers of fear and walls of self-protection may seem to block this love from flowing in or flowing out, but these walls can be made transparent by deeply inquiring into their nature. We can ask whether the Love we are actually needs protection. We can begin to heal ourselves of the need to stay defended by being willing to consciously experience what created the fear, instead of simply trying to control life, or our own feelings, so that we never have to experience what was painful again.

We are so conditioned to go to the mind of thought to tell us what to do, what to feel, how to act. But thought does not know how to love. Only our true Heart can love, and it moves with both wisdom and compassion simultaneously. This is not a blind emotionality; it contains a deep wisdom. Love is not blind. Unlike our attachments, it sees clearly.

Ultimately we may discover that Love moves life. It needs no reason; it simply loves TO BE. Being is "being" everything out of its infinite love and freedom. What if we incarnated to BE love in this world? What if we are here to touch with love all of the unloved parts of ourselves and our world, to gather everything back into the wholeness of being, the truth of what we are? Can we see clearly that to truly love means to die to separation?

WHAT CAN BE SAID ABOUT LOVE?

What can be said about love?
Nothing, really.
We are either being love
or we're talking about it.
Talk is cheap; love can't be bought.

It is not about flowery words,
or the agony or ecstasy of emotion.
It is not even about relationship,
or merging union with the Divine.
Where are there two?

And yet…and yet…
This wordless pull of connection—
even when the mind
wants no connection.
What is that unsought warmth?

That melting of resistance,
the fire that makes
even iron turn to liquid,
or a caterpillar dissolve
before wings emerge?

Love's only true language is Being.
Demand love, and it will flee.
Bargain with love, and you will lose.
Eventually, you will rejoice in defeat;
Love refuses all separation.

Love moves, responds, touches,
returns the unwanted pieces of your life
back to wholeness. Its language is truth,
and truth speaks love, but these are words,
and not alive, until your heart opens.

Every moment love is gently knocking
from inside, longing to flow out;
but we are busy looking elsewhere,
searching in the market place of "me's"
to fill the emptiness that is, itself, vast love.

What can be said about love?
Nothing, really. These words fail.
We are either being love
or we're talking about it.
Choose the former, if you have a choice,
for love alone transforms.

I AM is neither personal nor impersonal.
It is the love-to-be.
Sheer existence is the expression of this love.
Form is created because You love to BE.
You do not care what shape, what color,
What length of existence or vastness of experience.
You simply love to BE.
You love to be a butterfly whose life lasts a single day.
You love to be a human being who might live 100 years.
Love is both your pleasure and your pain.

⁊

Caring with attachment is human;
Caring without attachment, divine.
Sometimes heads, sometimes tails;
What notices which side is up?

⁊

In true Love, there is no opposite called hate.
There are no opposites at all.

⁊

Heaven is not a future.
It is your present when there is love.

The common thread in all true faith is love.
Love knows no division.
How, therefore, can division be made in the name of love?

Do you want love,
or do you want control?

Why else has the One
divided itself in Two
if not to Love Itself in expression?

Love is Being
Love is Presence
Love is Truth

In this choiceless
never-ending
flow
of life,
there is an infinite array
of choices.
One alone
brings happiness –
to love
what is.

When giver and receiver are One,
Love completes itself.

Love neither argues nor capitulates.
It has no agenda except loving.

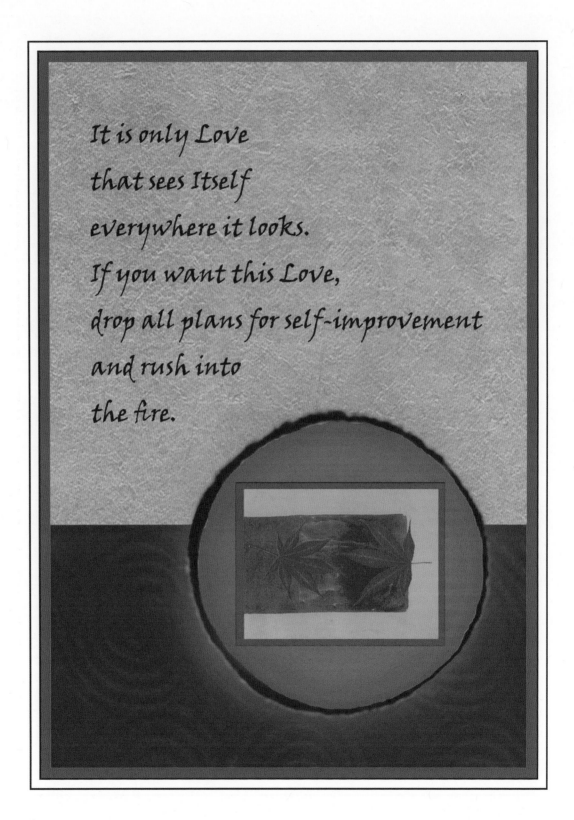

It is only Love
that sees Itself
everywhere it looks.
If you want this Love,
drop all plans for self-improvement
and rush into
the fire.

106

UNDRESS YOUR HEART

Remove the bulletproof vest
that has been covering your heart.
Rather than protecting you,
it is the cause of pain.

Undress your heart!
You have imprisoned Love.
No wonder it aches!
Its longing is a message.

Let Love's tiny stirrings
become an explosion
that shatters Separation.
Love needs no protector.

Its ocean is your body.
Its sun melts frozen sorrow.
It sword cuts through delusion.
Its tenderness heals wounds.

Undress your heart!
Let yourself fall open
in your longing
to What ends longing.

The Unborn tugs Itself
playfully, sharply, mysteriously,
with utmost love.

To open,
to receive,
to surrender
Separation—
An intimate kiss
from Love Itself.

୬

The river of my longing
reversed course; its currents
returned to the Heart.
Now there is nowhere to go.

I stand alone, the source
and the fulfillment
of all my desires.
Longing lit the pathway
Home.

୬

Until you have fully embraced
your humanity
without relinquishing your
divinity,
you have not come Home.

How seductive

the kiss

of Presence,

undressing layers of mind
until the heart peers out!

110

ON THE BIRTH OF A NEW YEAR

We have all been given a terminal diagnosis.
It is called birth. Here, on the birth
of a new year that will manifest
as-yet-unknown moments,
let us remember our Stillness
that rests untouched, yet embraces
birth and death,
sickness and health,
goodness and evil,
past and future,
heaven and earth.

Before the world was divided,
it was whole.
Now that it is divided, it is still whole.
Remember your wholeness!
It excludes nothing;
not one moment stands outside.
Before hatred was born,
Love created Life. Now,
even in the midst of pain,
fear, revenge, war, uncertainty,
Love still lives!

Love abides above and below,
beside and between, and
without exception, within
the seen and unseen worlds.
Skin may wrinkle, organs may fail
as the body moves inexorably
from birth to death.
But what never fails, and never dies
is Love, Love unconditioned
by thought, mood, emotion, story.

Love, beyond liking or disliking,
beyond our petty judgments,
beyond our fearful hearts
and fearful minds that
look for sympathy, approval
or a business arrangement
rather than opening to Love.
This year, may we all deeply
receive this Love, this Truth,
this Stillness that never suffers,
yet compassionately touches what does.

Ending is the destiny
for all that begins.

And for the beginningless?

Birth & Death

A LEAF FALLS IN AUTUMN. It returns to the ground, provides mulch for the tree that remains during all seasons. We do not imagine the leaf falling is a tragedy, do we? We see the cycle of life, and know that birth and death are simply happenings in Life. Such happenings are not separate from Life, and not separate from the ground of our Being. Yet, when a human body is returned to its Ground, we often see such an appearance as a failure—a failure of medicine, a failure of the person, a failure of God. We live in a culture that seems afraid to look at death with clear and loving eyes.

However, when we deeply understand that the essential nature of reality is without separation, we begin to have a different relationship with the "appearance" of birth and death. The Unborn is beyond any notions of coming or going, being or non-being, and yet continually flows as Life itself, transforming its infinite expressions according to causes and conditions.

While the experiences called birth and death happen each moment, and call forth many different responses, in Reality, separation does not exist. By letting go and dying into the present moment, we continually find Life's fullness and its great mystery.

Our true nature is the nature of no birth and no death, and it is only in touching our true nature that we can be free of the notions that anything begins from nothing or dies into nothing. It is true that cells are continually coming into being and dying off. Each breath, thought, feeling, and experience are arising and ending. Bodies, trees, leaves, flowers, clouds move in and out of form, yet Life continues endlessly.

We imagine a "me" is born and a "me" will die. But who is this me? Is this body not made up of millions of ever-birthing, ever-dying cells? Of the genetic matter of our ancestors? Of the water and food that sustain us? Of the sunshine and soil that produce our food? Of the myriad experiences that we link together and call a "self"? But we do not remain the same in two consecutive moments—neither does the river, or a cloud. The only thing that remains the same is the Awareness within which all of life is happening, including the happenings called birth and death.

We do not resolve the great matter of birth, life and death by denying birth and death, or trying to transcend them, but by thoroughly accepting the movement of life, the movement of the moment, knowing what is moving, birthing and dying.

Can we make friends with the body's impermanence, with the impermanence of all form, and yet remain conscious of That which is continually here regardless of the experiences that come and go? If there were no apparent impermanence, there could be no movement of life, breath, creation, or transformation. Even impermanence is only "apparent," since life is only continuing, always and everywhere—matter changing into energy, energy into matter, timeless being experienced as time, life flowing as a manifestation of an infinite Reality.

With the birth of my children, unconditional love seemed to leap into form. Many years later at the birth of my first grandson, I tenderly watched his head being born and knew in that very moment, death was being born as well. More recently, I was present at the death of my husband. It was a peaceful transition that ended any fear of death that might have lingered in the mind. That is not to say that the experiences of his illness, treatment, eventual hospitalization, and subsequent death were not challenging.

Living awake does not mean there will be no challenges or no grief. Grief is an expression of love in these human forms. When it is allowed to move freely without judgment and without suppression, it is a gift that appears when it does, and disappears when it does, itself being birthed and dying back into Love.

What has been so amazing is that I feel no separation from the spirit that was my husband, the spirit that we all are, and so I see that spirit everywhere I look. I see my husband, not as form, but as formless: as the vast sky, the hummingbirds that hover nearby, the leaves on Moon Mountain, in the faces of all of us who loved him deeply. I see that what he truly was, he still Is.

Death has invited an even more palpable remembrance of our true nature. Grief transforms into gratitude. And the love we experienced during our 54 years together has only grown beyond any identification with form. There are many sweet memories of our life together in form. I miss his laughter, his touch, his particular expression of the Love we are, but deeper still is the felt-sense of No Separation. And because I do not sense separation in the Now, I do not fantasize about a "meeting" place in the great beyond. Here and Now is where we meet; in fact, it is where we have always been One.

Love is much stronger than any idea of love, and stronger than any notion of death. Love embraces life in the form we call "birth," and in the form we call "death." Death pertains to the body, yet from the deepest realization of our true nature, nothing is born and nothing has died. Forms take shape, appear to be born and appear to die, but the essence of all is Unborn.

There are many forms of dying and being born. We deaden ourselves daily by trying to put life in a conceptual box and hold on to it as a construct instead of as a living, breathing moving whole. Can we die to the last moment and live in this one?

116

By learning to die into the present, we open ourselves to Life. Life in form sometimes holds moments of grief or sadness or pain; but it also holds moments of liberation and joy in letting go into the Deathless spirit that we are.

Here in the center
of your sweet birth is death—
not other, not separate,
not somewhere yet to be.
Death itself comes with this moment
of your head birthing itself.
But beyond birth and death,
Love is born anew.

There is no arrival at birth,
no departure at death.
Where would I come from?
Where would I go?
Where could the Undivided
Enter or exit?

These pink clouds
are innocent,
yet they are dying.
They gave their life
for this moment.
Now the wind
disperses them.
So too, this cloud we call our
life.

In the deep Ocean of compassion,
moonlight falls as tears
in the midst of pain!

Death may invite you to swim
to the bottom of grief.
There is always a surprise
waiting at the bottom!

To be gripped by the certainty of death
and still love: Is not this love
your innocence?

See if facing death does not
Invite you to live in a way
Nothing else can or ever will.

Death comes as illusion;
Life comes as illusion.
What will end illusion?
Death.
The only thing that dies is illusion.

THE FRIENDLINESS OF DEATH

Here, right behind the next television show
The next new age healing machine
The next mantram
The next guru
The next emotional enlightenment game
The next cathartic opening
The next insight about your past
The next version of your favorite car
The next computer game
The next download
The next sweet circle of well-meaning egos
The next therapy for body, mind, and soul
The next crystal for chakra balancing
The next technique for discovering Nothing
Sits a great friend you consider foe:
Death.
See if facing death does not
Invite you to live in a way
Nothing else can or ever will.
Death comes as illusion;
Life comes as illusion.
What will end illusion?
Death.
The only thing that dies is illusion.

As the mind imagined a thousand deaths,
I simply slipped out the side door
and left mind to its dreaming.

THIS BODY IS A TENT

This body is a tent—
a tent set up on desert sands
where winds blow through
and rustle coverings
but cannot be contained,
no matter how the tent is made.

Beautiful silks may fly in the breeze,
or be drenched in desert sorrows;
one day the tent will surely collapse,
yet still the winds will never stop;
so why do you grieve a piece of cloth
when you could be the wind?

A VAST WARDROBE

Look how this nakedness shows its vast wardrobe!
Here it dresses as a rose;
there it dresses as a car;
here the suit is Mother;
there the suit is Daughter.
Spirit does not inhabit these things.
Nothingness does not climb in and out.
The rose grows thorns
and does not bloom in winter;
the mother will one day sleep without waking
and her daughter will weep.

When my eyes close, and
can no longer see the moon,
the Moon will have liberated
this form from its limitations.
Weep, if you must, for yourselves,
but do not weep for me.

Sometimes grief comes gently,
like a butterfly landing on your hand,
reminding you that life is here,
even if he isn't.

Sometimes it comes violently,
like a torrential downpour,
washing away everything
you once cared about.

Sometimes it wells up
in the morning when the place
beside you in the bed you shared
feels cold and empty.

Sometimes it's made of
happy memories you cherish
that make you so very grateful
for the years you spent together.

Sometimes it dissipates
as quickly as it comes, as you
watch water rivulets glide slowly
down the shower door.

Sometimes it buries your
face in his robe still hanging
where he left it, and you are
cradled by his familiar scent.

Sometimes it surrounds
your morning cup of tea
as you picture him sitting where
he always sat across from you.

And sometimes it vanishes altogether,
and life is full again,
and you are full again,
and free of dreams.

ON THE DEATH OF MY HUSBAND

My husband has transformed himself.
He is not gone but comes now
as the flowing fountain, bubbles
in the stream, the great vast ocean,
graceful olive trees,
and sturdy oaks.

He flies to me as a hummingbird,
wings shaping the sign of infinity,
inviting me to See deeply.
He hops about on the lush green
grass as his favorite bird,
a robin.

At first, he came so powerfully,
almost in a human form,
squeezing my hand, awakening
me from slumber, lying in bed
beside me, or sitting next
to me on a park bench.

But now his soul's journey no longer
hovers in a familiar form.
How can I grieve his freedom?
How can I wish him back
into a sick body?
I do not.

I miss his touch, his laugh,
his generous spirit calling me
to love more deeply;
but these now live inside my heart,
this single Heart we share
with all creation.

My beloved has not departed;
I feel his spirit everywhere I look.
It blows as the wind
that kisses my cheek.
It tastes my tears and
smiles at my joy.

No, my husband is not gone;
but merely transformed,
as we all will be one day,
returned to the formless
Spirit we are, even now, in these
fragile, yet resilient forms.

Death is not an end, but
a beginning of a deeper
love, a deeper freedom,
a deeper joy that
confirms this truth:
There simply is No Separation.

Where would I go?
Where could the Undivided
Enter or exit?

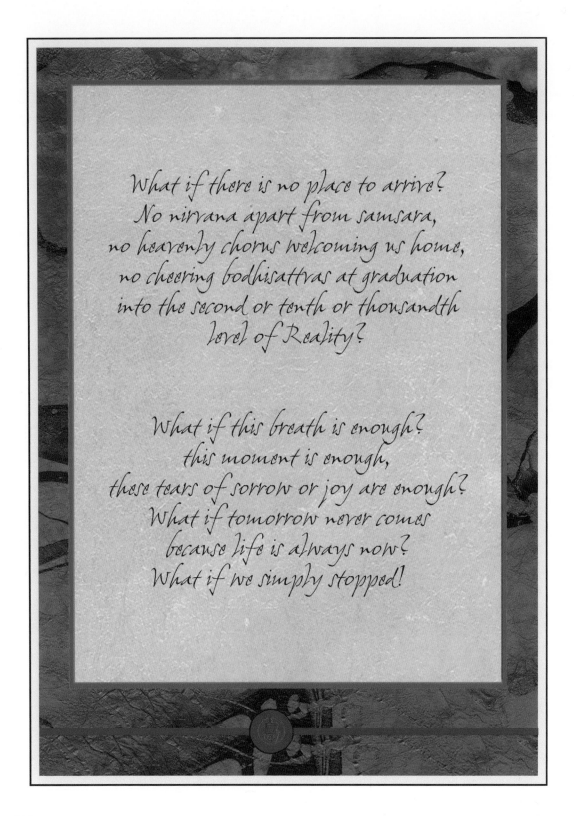

What if there is no place to arrive?
No nirvana apart from samsara,
no heavenly chorus welcoming us home,
no cheering bodhisattvas at graduation
into the second or tenth or thousandth
level of Reality?

What if this breath is enough?
this moment is enough,
these tears of sorrow or joy are enough?
What if tomorrow never comes
because life is always now?
What if we simply stopped!

Now

EVERY SINGLE EXPERIENCE WE HAVE EVER HAD HAS OCCURRED IN THE NOW, has it not? Yet Now is neither a split second in time, that could always be divisible, nor is it an eternity imagined to be an endless duration in time.

Now is the infinite timelessness of Being. When Now is seen through the mind, it is called Time, but Now is actually the absence of time. Experientially, we might say it is where time and the timeless collapse into each other. When attention is placed in the Now, subject and object also collapse, and there is an intimacy with experience, a stillness, an alive presence. The present experience seems fresh and vivid because we are seeing it through the eyes of the timeless Awareness that we are.

Now is the entry point to the timeless. When we touch truth, there is no time. Our minds can only live in time, but when we touch the Now, we move out of the time-bound confines of thought and conditioning. The present moment is the only moment we can experience the flow of life, and the only moment we can live awake. It is the entry point to liberation. Living now is not living "then" or "when." Past and future dissolve in the experience of Now. Living now is our freedom.

Can we sense our own awareness intimately touch itself as a cloud, a tree, a feeling, a word, a human being? What happens when we stop moving away from the experience that already IS, neither holding on to beauty nor pushing away fear, but letting the moment be as it is and move as it does? This action takes us out of thought, judgment and narrative for a moment, and returns us to our awake presence, that is always Now.

Our own inherent awake nature is open to the moment as it is. Past is memory and future a projection, a movement of thought. Both may occur in the present moment, but neither are the Reality of Now. Awareness is simply here for what is here now. That is its freedom, and its peace.

Are *You* only your body, thoughts, feelings and perceptions, that are continually changing? Or are you more deeply and truly the timeless awake, aware Presence that notices thoughts, feelings, sensations, perceptions as they occur?

We can only be awake Now. When what is ceaselessly Awake within us moves through mind, it births time; when it moves through perception, it births space with its myriad forms. Whether the moment appears to be an infant taking her first breath, or an old woman exhaling her last—never for a single moment is life, or its appearances, separate from what is whole, undivided, and awake Now.

PEACE IS THIS MOMENT WITHOUT JUDGMENT

Do you think peace requires an end to war?
Or tigers eating only vegetables?
Does peace require an absence
from your boss, your spouse, yourself?
Do you think peace will come some other place than here?
Some other time than Now?
In some other heart than yours?

Peace is this moment without judgment.
That is all. This moment in the Heart-space
where everything that is is welcome.
Peace is this moment without thinking
that it should be some other way,
that you should feel some other thing,
that your life should unfold according to your plans.

Peace is this moment without judgment,
this moment in the Heart-space where
everything that is is welcome.

Time and no time collapse into Now.
You and other collapse into Now.
What remains?

ა

Leap free of yesterday's prison;
Breathe the fresh, green scent of Now.

ა

Heaven and hell vanish tasting Now.

ა

Call off the search!
Behold the miracle of
your ordinary life,
the precious gift of Now.

TOO LONG

Too long have we considered
the drama, the journey,
the seriousness of seeking,
the victory of finding,
the great pretense that
eyes must strain to truly See.

Too long have we followed
the continual scanning
of mind for bruises, flaws,
neurotic tendencies, the
great need for self-improvement
for a self that doesn't exist!

Too long have we been striving
to be always more perfect—
perfectly free, perfectly healthy,
perfectly realized,
perfect embodiment of truth,
perfect puppet of spiritual ego!

It's time to dance with joy,
to spread our wings and fly,
to relish each moment of living
without judgment of whether
it should or should not be
what it clearly is!

Let's fall on our faces in the mud,
and lick the earth off our lips!
Let's smile at the next person we see.
Let's stop pursuing and start receiving
the fullness of this life,
the only one that's happening.

Too long have we indulged the
frightened one, standing on the shore,
afraid of drowning in a sea of love,
afraid to let go of old grievances,
old habit patterns of mind
that have not delivered what we'd hoped.

What if there is no place to arrive?
No nirvana apart from samsara,
no heavenly chorus welcoming us home,
no cheering bodhisattvas at graduation
into the second or tenth or thousandth
level of Reality?

What if this breath is enough?
this moment is enough,
these tears of sorrow or joy are enough?
What if tomorrow never comes
because life is always now?
What if we simply stopped!

ONLY THIS MOMENT

Only this moment of our friendship,
this moment of intimate meeting.
In meeting, we meet the ancestors,
the buddhas, and all sentient beings.

We meet the clouds of dawn
and the clear summer sky.
We taste pure mountain rain
and the ocean's salty waves.

We meet where nothing has ever met
yet continually greets itself with tenderness.
We meet without a face, yet here is a smile.
There is nothing to teach; yet compassion moves;

Nothing to transmit, yet being vibrates;
no place to go, yet each moment arrives.
The songbird sings his heart
out of each listening ear.

Beloved Friend of eons too vast to speak,
limitless Beneficence pours itself an endless sea,
then swims in its own gratitude. Nothing happens,
yet this overflowing of nothing is able to quench

the deepest thirst. Meeting where there is no meeting,
illusions are seen to be clear buddha nature
at last, and there is nothing but this moment,
this moment of our intimate meeting.

Acknowledgments

I WANT TO EXPRESS MY DEEP APPRECIATION for the support, love, and beautiful artwork provided by Rashani Réa, whose interest and enthusiasm for this book provided great inspiration for its completion. Rashani and I met on a bus ride to the Rocky Mountains to attend a retreat with Thich Nhat Hanh in 1989. While our paths have not crossed often since then, we have shared a love of both the dharma and one another's presence in this world. The creative spirit simply pours through Rashani in so many amazing ways—her devotion to truth, to caring for the earth, to being a healing presence to those whose lives have been touched by sorrow or injustice, together with her openness to her crafts as artist, songwriter and poet, in her own right.

Beside me in life and beyond his death, I would also like to express my deepest love, tenderness and unfathomable gratitude for my late husband, Jim, whose love, humor, and generosity over our more than 50 years together remain continual daily reminders that Love is much stronger than death. The Spirit that he is, that you and I are, knows no Separation. The transition we call death simply calls us to remember more deeply our Oneness with one another, with all beings, with all of life.

Others have shown the way of No Separation as well. I will be forever indebted to the appearance of Ramana Maharshi in my life, to the path of self-inquiry, and to Adyashanti—a living Buddha, true Friend and teacher, whose compassion, clarity, and love have become permanently embedded in my heart.

To my wise and wonderful children, grandchildren, clients, students, friends, and Sangha members, know that you have been teachers every step of the way as well, and I feel such a full and grateful heart for each one of you.

Special thanks go to the Board of Moon Mountain Sangha for their encouragement and support of this book project, to Ali Miller and Julia Hunt Nielsen for their editing skills, and to Cindy Chang, whose design expertise contributed greatly to the production of this book.

Lastly, it is Moon Mountain that continually invites silence and deep gratitude. Leaves bud, unfurl, change colors, and are returned to the Ground as seasons shift on the mountain and in our own lives. Yet each moment fully and completely reflects the infinite Mystery that moves life. May you and all beings awaken beyond appearances to the Light that shines in every form, including your own.

Notes

Should you be interested in obtaining any of the collages in this book or many others in Rashani's collection of cards and posters, you may visit www.rashani.com

About the Author

DOROTHY HUNT serves as spiritual director of Moon Mountain Sangha, teaching at the request and in the spiritual lineage of Adyashanti. She is the founder of the San Francisco Center for Meditation and Psychotherapy and has practiced psychotherapy since 1967. Dorothy is the author of *Only This!*, and a contributing author to both *The Sacred Mirror: Nondual Wisdom and Psychotherapy*, vol.1, and *Listening from the Heart of Silence: Nondual Wisdom and Psychotherapy*, vol.2. as well as the online journal, *Undivided*. Her poetry has appeared in a number of journals, and she is a featured spiritual teacher in the book, *Ordinary Women, Extraordinary Wisdom*. Dorothy has a long and deep connection with the teachings of Ramana Maharshi, the path of self-inquiry, and the nondual teachings of Zen, Advaita, and the Christian mystics. She offers satsang, retreats, and private meetings in the San Francisco Bay Area, and elsewhere by invitation.

www.dorothyhunt.org

About the Artist

RASHANI RÉA is the founder of Kipukamaluhia, a Dharma-Gaia sanctuary on the Big Island of Hawai'i. For nearly thirty years she has offered concerts, councils, and retreats throughout the world, sharing her passion for "Soetry" (song and poetry), deep ecology, earth-based spirituality, Buddhist and Process-oriented psychology, the Direct Approach, and what she calls "The Pathless Journey." In celebration of the diversity of Timeless Wisdom, Rashani has published 14 books and recorded 15 albums, including *Take Refuge in the Moment, Songs of Interbeing, Only Grace Remains,* and *Death is a Gateway.*

www.rashani.com

Printed in Great Britain
by Amazon